Wild Weather

Hurricane

REVISED AND UPDATED

Heinemann
LIBRARY

Catherine Chambers

www.heinemann.co.uk/library
Visit our website to find out more information about **Heinemann Library** books.

To order:
☎ Phone ++44 (0)1865 888112
▤ Send a fax to ++44 (0)1865 314091
💻 Visit the Heinemann Bookshop at www.heinemann.co.uk/library to browse our catalogue and order online.

First published in Great Britain by Heinemann Library, Halley Court, Jordan Hill, Oxford OX2 8EJ, part of Harcourt Education. Heinemann is a registered trademark of Harcourt Education.

Editorial: Clare Lewis
Designed: Steve Mead and Q2A
Illustrations: Paul Bale
Picture Research: Tracy Cummins
Production: Julie Carter

Originated by Modern Age Repro
Printed and bound in China by South China Printing Company Limited

10 digit ISBN 0 431 15086 9
13 digit ISBN 978 0 431 15086 4

11 10 09 08 07
10 9 8 7 6 5 4 3 2 1

British Library Cataloguing in Publication Data

Chambers, Catherine
Wild Weather: Hurricane. – 2nd Edition – Juvenile literature
551.5'52
A full catalogue record for this book is available from the British Library.

Acknowledgements
The Publishers would like to thank the following for permission to reproduce photographs: AP Photo/Mark Saltz/STR p22, Associated Press pp4, 9, 13, Corbis pp5, 11, 20, 24, 27, 29, James Nielsen/AFP/Getty Images p23, PA Photos p21, Panos p28, Photodisc p25, Joe Raedle/Getty Images p18, Reuters/Corbis p14, Rex Features pp15, 19, 26, Robert Harding Picture Library p12, Royalty Free/Corbis pp7, 16, Science Photo Library p10, Mar Torres/AFP/Getty Images p17.

Cover photograph of palm trees during Hurricane Wilma in 2005 reproduced with permission of Daniel Aguilar/Reuters/Corbis.

The Publishers would like to thank Mark Rogers and the Met Office for their assistance with the preparation of this book.

Every effort has been made to contact copyright holders of any material reproduced in this book. Any omissions will be rectified in subsequent printings if notice is given to the Publisher.

The paper used to print this book comes from sustainable resources.

Any words appearing in the text in bold, **like this**, are explained in the Glossary.

Contents

What is a hurricane?

A hurricane is a huge storm that builds up over the **oceans**. Strong winds hit the land. Swirling clouds bring heavy rain.

■ *The wind is very strong in a hurricane.*

■ *Hurricanes can cause a lot of damage.*

Hurricane winds blow roofs off and smash windows. They snap trees and flatten **crops**. Streets and homes can be flooded by heavy rain or huge waves from the sea.

Where do hurricanes happen?

Hurricanes happen in a region called the **Tropics**. The Tropics are hot because the heat of the Sun is stronger in this region. Hurricanes are called "typhoons" in some places.

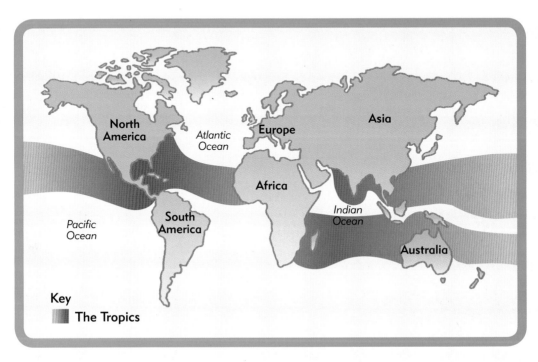

Key
The Tropics

■ *The areas in blue on this map show where hurricanes happen.*

■ *This country lies in a **hurricane zone**.*

This place lies in the Tropics. Very strong hurricanes happen here because it is close to warm **oceans**. Warm oceans help hurricanes to form.

How do hurricanes form?

Masses of air are always moving. A warm mass of air usually rises. This makes a low **pressure** area. A cold mass sinks. This makes high pressure. Winds blow from high pressure to low pressure.

■ *This diagram shows how masses of air are moved by the wind.*

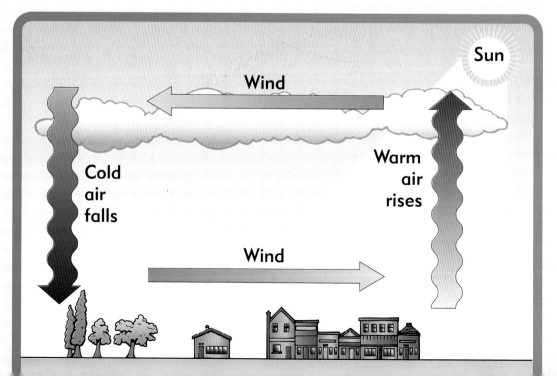

■ *This photograph shows a hurricane from space.*

Hurricanes happen when air rises quickly over warm **oceans** in the **Tropics**. This makes a low pressure area. Strong winds rush in from high pressure areas. They form a **spiral** of wind and clouds around an area of still air.

What do hurricanes do?

Hurricanes form over the **ocean**. Hurricane winds are very powerful. The winds blow the sea into huge waves. Heavy rain falls from huge, dark clouds.

■ *Hurricanes can damage boats at sea.*

■ *Houses on the coast can be in danger.*

Hurricanes blow on to tropical **coasts**. As a hurricane blows over the land it gets less powerful. The hurricane can still do a lot of damage.

What are hurricanes like?

Hurricane winds blow through towns and cities. They uproot trees and blow the roofs off buildings. It is too windy for people to go outside.

■ *It is dangerous to go outside in a hurricane.*

■ *The heavy rain can flood roads.*

Hurricanes bring heavy rain. They drop the water they have picked up from the **ocean** on to the land. This can often cause **floods**.

Harmful hurricanes

A hurricane **storm surge** has hit this **shore**. The surge is a huge wave pushed by the strong wind. The wave **floods** the shore. These boats have been carried on to the land.

■ *These boats have been damaged by a hurricane.*

■ *This airport has been destroyed.*

Hurricanes damage roads, railways, bridges, and airports. This makes it difficult for rescuers to reach people after a hurricane.

Hurricane in Mexico

This is Cancun in Mexico. Cancun lies in the warm Caribbean Sea. People go there on holiday. Mexico gets a lot of hurricanes.

■ *People love to go to the beach in Cancun when the weather is good.*

■ *This building was destroyed by a hurricane in 2005.*

In 2005, Hurricane Wilma damaged hotels and shops. People could not stay here on holiday. This harmed Mexico's **tourist industry**.

Preparing for a hurricane

Weather forecasters can see a hurricane forming and moving in photos taken by **satellites** in space. The hurricane's cloud moves in a **spiral** over the Earth.

■ *This woman is checking the latest satellite photos to see if a hurricane is forming.*

Television, radio, and the Internet warn people before the hurricane strikes. On the **coast**, officers from the **emergency services** use special flags to warn people that a hurricane is on the way.

■ *Red flags can warn people to find safety.*

Coping with hurricanes

People fix strong wooden boards to doors and windows before a hurricane strikes. This stops things blown by the hurricane from smashing the windows.

■ *People protect their homes when they know a hurricane is coming.*

■ *It is sometimes safer to leave home before a hurricane hits.*

Many people go to community halls or special **shelters** before the hurricane hits. They are given food and a place to sleep. They stay until the hurricane is over and it is safe to go home.

Hurricane winds and rain can destroy **crops**. In poor countries such as Bangladesh these crops are very important. If they are destroyed, people will not have enough to eat.

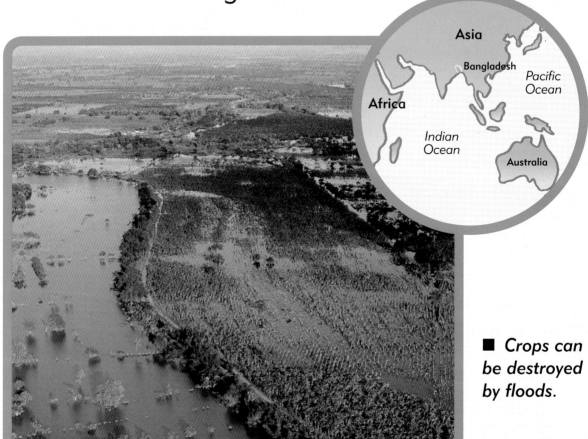

Asia

Bangladesh

Pacific Ocean

Africa

Indian Ocean

Australia

■ *Crops can be destroyed by floods.*

■ *Palm trees are designed to survive hurricanes.*

Palm trees grow in the **Tropics**. These trees can bend and sway. This stops them from breaking in a hurricane.

Adapting to hurricanes

Belize is a country in Central America. A hurricane destroyed its **capital city**, which lay on the **coast**. This picture shows the new city.

■ *The new city was built inland, well away from hurricanes.*

Asia

Pacific
Ocean

Africa

Indian
Ocean

Australia

■ *Buildings in a hurricane zone must be specially designed.*

Parts of Australia lie in a **hurricane zone**.
People now have to build stronger buildings
to protect them from hurricanes.

Fact file

The worst known hurricane disaster happened in the country of Bangladesh in 1970. About 500,000 people died.

◆ There is a small area of still air in the centre of a hurricane. This place is called the "eye" of the storm.

Hurricanes are given names such as Shane or Tamsin. Their names go in alphabetical order. They go in order of boy and girl, too.

Glossary

aid workers workers who help people in a disaster

capital city most important city of any country

coasts where the land meets the sea

crops plants grown for food

disease illness

emergency services people who help us when there is a disaster, for example the police, ambulance, and fire services.

flood overflowing water

hurricane zone area where hurricanes often happen

mass huge area or amount of something

oceans vast areas of sea

pressure pushing force

satellite spacecraft that moves around the Earth

shelters safe places

shore where the sea meets the land

spiral winding round and round

storm surge huge sea wave pushed to the shore by hurricane winds

tourist industry when people pay to visit places and attractions on holiday

Tropics very warm areas of the world near the Equator. The Equator is an imaginary line around the fattest part of Earth.

weather forecasters scientists who work out what the weather will be like

More Books to read

Weather Watch: *Wind*, Honor Head (QED, 2006).

The Weather: *Wind*, Angela Royston (Chrysalis Children's Books, 2004).

Index

Titles in the *Wild Weather* series include:

Hardback 978-0-431-15081-9

Hardback 978-0-431-15082-6

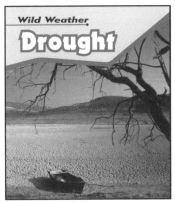

Hardback 978-0-431-15083-3

Hardback 978-0-431-15080-2

Hardback 978-0-431-15085-7

Hardback 978-0-431-15086-4

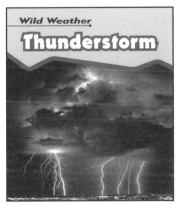

Hardback 978-0-431-15087-1

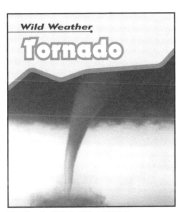

Hardback 978-0-431-15088-8

Find out about other titles Heinemann Library on our website www.heinemann.co.uk/library